Natural Ideas
for Christmas

*Fantastic
decorations
to make*

Natural Ideas
for Christmas

Fantastic decorations to make

Josie Cameron-Ashcroft
and Carol Cox

Guild of Master Craftsman Publications Ltd

First published 1999 by
Guild of Master Craftsman Publications Ltd,
166 High Street, Lewes,
East Sussex, BN7 1XU

ISBN 1 86108 132 4

Photographs (and cover photography) by Martin Sookias
© All photographs Josie Cameron-Ashcroft
All rights reserved

A catalogue record for this book is available from the British
Library

The publishers and authors can accept no legal responsibility for
any consequences arising from the application of information,
advice or instructions given in this publication.
Designed by Teresa Dearlove
Cover design by Wheelhouse Design
Typeface: Simoncini Garamond
Colour origination by Viscan Graphics (Singapore)
Printed and bound by Kyodo Printing (Singapore) under the
supervision of MRM Graphics, Winslow, Buckinghamshire UK

ACKNOWLEDGEMENTS

Carol and Josie would like to thank the following people whose expertise, patience and
encouragement made this book possible. In particular Joanna Cooke-Yarborough for her
tremendous patience sitting through hours of photo shoots so ably and willingly modelling
hands, with her unfailing sense of humour. Martin Sookias for his superb photography.
Woody Lenton for his willing help and extremely clever ideas. Alan, Sue and all at Alagar,
New Covent Garden Flower Market, London for putting aside all those little gems so early
in the morning. Stephanie Horner, Cath Laing and all the professional team at the Guild of
Master Craftsman for bringing this book together. Michael for holding the fort on so many
occasions and for being there.

For Georgina, Bex, Woody, Edward, Henry and Lucy

Contents

Introduction 1

Essential equipment 2

Sourcing materials 6

Essential techniques 16
Adding colour • Drying fruits • Wiring fruits,
cones and pots • Cutting foliage • Candles
Sticks and twigs • Mossing a rope • Mossing a welcome ring

Ribbons and bows 34
Raffia knots • Twig bow • Ribbons • Rosebuds
Cheat's bows • Double petal bows

Projects

Garlands
Traditional Christmas garland 46
Silver twig garland 50
Gilded ivy garland 53

Welcome rings
Traditional Christmas welcome ring 56
Silver twig ring 60
Gilded ivy ring 63

Buckets and logs
Thistle urn 66
Lily bucket 69
Yuletide log 71

Table centrepieces
Gold nut pot 74
Mandarin and pine cone centrepiece 77
Christmas rose loaf 80
Christmas name places 83

Candles
Vine leaf candles 85
Ivy and pomegranate candle 87
Christmas hydrangea pot 90
Rose and ivy candle 94

Christmas trees
Shaker tree 97
Silver twig tree 100

Chairbacks
Mandarin and nut ball chairback 103
Evergreen berry, fruit and cone chairback 107

Gifts for unexpected visitors 110

About the authors 114

Index 115

Introduction

Christmas is a wonderful and exciting occasion when we look forward to decorating our homes, both inside and out, with welcoming and cheerful arrangements. We have written this book in order that you can do just that with minimal effort and maximum effect. You will be able to create professional-looking arrangements, with a few simple ingredients, in the comfort of your own home.

The art of natural Christmas decoration is explained here in easy-to-follow recipes, just like in a cook book. Using rustic themes and natural ingredients, enhanced with gold and silver, the aim is to add glamour and magic to your home. Favourite recipes can be dipped into year after year.

Think big, think dramatic and make striking statements with your arrangements. For example, if you like the idea of forest fruits such as pine cones, mosses and nuts adorning your table, gather together many more ingredients than you think you need. With an abundance of materials you will be able to create a wonderfully solid,

substantial arrangement from which you and your family and friends will derive great pleasure

Group materials together for impact. For example, instead of using single pine cones, use bulky groups of threes, fives or sevens; odd numbers work best. Confidence is all you need, together with some useful tricks of the trade, which we will provide in the following techniques and projects.

We will suggest colour combinations, for instance, mix exquisite pinks and reds with oranges and golds. You can experiment, using your own colour preferences and blending tones. Follow your instincts whilst applying the basic rules of thumb suggested in this book. Most of the projects shown in this book are quick and easy to make, so roll up your sleeves, get on with the tasks described, and above all, enjoy it.

Remember, there is no right or wrong way to arrange natural ingredients. Just stick to a couple of simple rules, don't be afraid to add your own ideas and you will be able to achieve a wonderful, colourful Christmas display every time.

Essential equipment

The list of equipment and tools you need will depend on how many of the projects you want to produce. There is a list of equipment for every project. It may, therefore, be worth selecting your projects before you rush out and buy anything. Most of the equipment listed is available from a flower shop, garden centre or a hardware store; where possible we have given homemade alternatives.

Chicken wire Either plastic coated or plain. Use with 1in (2.5cm) mesh if possible.

Collection of stub wires Available from flower shops and garden centres, these come in different gauges or thicknesses. The projects use mainly medium and heavy-gauge wire.

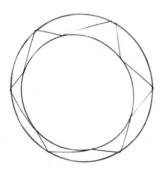

Circular 12–14in (30–36cm) diameter wire ring You can buy this from flower shops or garden centres.

Reel wire This is also called mossing wire and is suitable for binding woody stems. It is frequently used in the projects which follow.

Wire pins You can make these by cutting fine or medium-gauge stub wires to approximately 3in (8cm) lengths and then bending them in half, but you will need a large number, even when working on a fairly small project. They can also be bought cheaply from flower shops or garden centres.

Spray paints Gold and silver are suitable seasonal colours. Try to buy floral paint which is specially designed for spraying flowers. Go for bright gold and silver as the colour is often soaked up by the materials.

Acrylic paints and a fine paint brush For decorating terracotta pots.

Twine or string Use the natural twine available from garden centres and not nylon string as this breaks through plant materials.

Foam blocks and balls
a Wet – green in colour, suitable for fresh materials.
b Dry – grey in colour, suitable for dry plant materials.
c Wet foam pans – available from flower shops or garden centres, are used as bases for chair backs. The end can be snapped off or used to tie the pan in place on the back of a chair.

Parcel string This, by contrast, should have a nylon base, which ensures that it does not stretch – important for blue pine garlands which are fairly heavy.

PVA glue and thick brush We use this to coat terracotta pots before painting to ensure a non-porous surface.

Florist's tape A durable, solid, green waterproof adhesive tape used for wiring candles and fixing foam in place. It must be used on a dry surface, but once stuck it can get wet without losing its stickiness.

Plastic berries Red and gold are suitable colours, very useful for brightening up foliage. By late December the natural berries may have been gobbled up by the birds! If placed randomly they can look natural.

Dry hard or plaster of Paris Dry hard is a clay and takes approximately 24 hours to set. Alternatively, mix plaster of Paris to a thick consistency with water and it will dry in approximately 15 minutes.

Gravel Use fairly fine gravel if you can. Pots can be weighed down with gravel instead of using plaster of Paris.

If you are learning to use a glue gun, wear close-fitting thick gloves to protect your hands. If you do inadvertently burn yourself with the gun, run the burn under cold water immediately.

Glue gun Two types of glue gun are readily available; one which produces very hot glue, and the low heat glue gun. The latter is used for delicate flowers, but generally the hot glue gun is the most versatile. Always work over an old wooden board to avoid drips or scalds in the wrong places.

Foam fix This is a waterproof type of Blu-Tack.

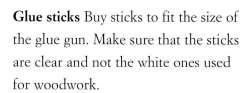

Glue sticks Buy sticks to fit the size of the glue gun. Make sure that the sticks are clear and not the white ones used for woodwork.

Candle holders Plastic candle holders are suitable for use in wet or dry foam. Make sure your candles are the correct size to fit, if not trim them to fit the holders. If none are available try wiring up the candle (see page 26).

Florist's scissors We recommend two pairs: one for cutting soft-stemmed flowers and ribbons, and the other for wires and hard-stemmed plant materials.

Sourcing materials

When choosing any natural ingredients look for good colour and freshness. For example, blue pine should have strong and springy needles and the cupressus needs to be a rich bright bluish-green. Avoid materials with any signs of limpness or fading. A blue pine door ring will last for weeks and weeks if the materials are fresh before you start. This is also true of the fruits. Make sure they are firm, under ripe if anything, and are beautifully coloured. You can afford to be choosy about natural materials because they are comparatively inexpensive.

Garden and hedgerow

You will be surprised at the range of foliage and flowers you can find in even the smallest garden. Hedgerows can produce all kinds of exciting finds: berries, fruits and seed heads.

Roses and hydrangeas can be expensive to buy, so it is well worth drying your own when they are in season. They look fabulous drying in bundles in the kitchen, tied at the bottom of their stems, hanging from a beam or hooks. They are decorations in themselves.

Holly will usually last a fairly long time if kept in fresh water, which should be changed regularly. The holly we have used in this book is the non-prickly variety. Holly can be very hard to work with if it has prickles – it sometimes just isn't worth the pain.

Ivy There are numerous species of ivies: variegated and plain, small and large leaved, star-shaped and rounded. Use a mixture of different types for a beautiful effect.

The birds enjoy holly as much as we do. If you have holly in your garden, tie netting around part of the bush to protect the berries from the birds until you are ready to cut it.

Evergreen foliage
Coniferous plants such as cupressus can be found in many gardens. Blue pine is more difficult to track down. It may be worth buying these types of foliage from a good florist's shop in order to ensure you have the best possible quality.

Pine cones and nuts Pine cones can be found in abundance in parks and woods. Cones which are more open are easier to wire up. Chestnuts, hazelnuts, pecans, walnuts and beech nuts can all be used to add colour, texture and shape to arrangements.

Mosses and lichens There are hundreds of different species of these, so do keep your eyes open. Even in busy city centres you can see moss growing on stone surfaces and between paving slabs. Most common mosses are considered weeds so few people will object to moss gatherers.

Sphagnum, carpet (also called flat moss) moss and lichen are the three types we would recommend. Ensure that moss is of good colour and fresh. If any moss you have gathered lacks lustre, spray it lightly with green paint of an appropriate shade.

Lichen can be bought dry from florist's shops. It is very crispy and needs to be soaked in boiling water. Leave it to cool and it will become soft, spongy, and ready to use.

Vine leaves Some varieties of vine turn a beautiful russet colour during autumn. If you are able to, collect these red-stained vine leaves in autumn, before they all drop on the ground and become marked. Once the moisture goes out of them, they will become too brittle to shape around the candles. So, think ahead, buy candles early, wrap them in vine leaves in the autumn and store them away in tissue paper.

Twigs It is easy to find twigs everywhere. Collect them early before the snow. Once gathered, sort the twigs into stems of similar thicknesses and trim off any side shoots. Tie them in bunches at the top and bottom for easy storage.

Beach and seaside

Collect shells and pebbles of all sorts –
flat, bumpy, speckled and sandbeaten.
Wash shells and pebbles carefully to
remove the salt and store in a jar or box
so that they don't get damaged. Shells
look beautiful if they are sprayed
different colours, or simply varnished
and allowed to dry, stacked at odd
angles on top of each other in a glass
bowl or vase.

Store cupboard

Store cupboards are marvellous places to rummage around at Christmas time. Get into the habit of keeping useful containers and decorative objects. For instance, old waste paper baskets can be covered with paper or papier-mâché or sprayed with paint to make stunning containers for decorations. An old clothes line which has been well weathered can be cut and wound around almost any container to give it a charm of its own. It is amazing how many items can be stacked one upon the other and stored using the minimum amount of space.

Terracotta pots These come in all sizes, from miniature to oversize (with drainage holes).

Galvanized buckets These can be used 'battered' or sprayed gold after being coated with PVA glue.

Loaf tins These come in a range of sizes, and can also be sprayed.

Jelly moulds Moulds come in a variety of shapes and sizes and are perfect for unusual arrangements.

Corks Old champagne corks can be used for decoration while ordinary corks can be used on the back of welcome rings, to protect your paintwork.

Glass vases, square and cylindrical These need to be of a fairly substantial size to allow another container to fit within them. Ideally the diameter of the container should be no smaller that 6in (15cm).

Glass or plastic jars to fit into pots and vases Look out for waterproof containers into which you can arrange flowers which cannot be put into foam because of their softness, hollowness or thickness. The container can be filled with water, packed with flowers and placed in a pretty vase. Any space between the inner and outer container can be filled with moss, pot pourri or beans to add interest.

Kitchen store cupboard

Take a completely different look at what you have in your kitchen and let your imagination go wild!

Nuts, seeds and pulses can be sprayed metallic colours or left partly natural.

Apples, mandarins, oranges and limes can be sliced and carefully dried (see page 20). They can also form decorations in their own right, piled high in glass containers or glued into slightly more sophisticated arrangements. Leeks and apples can be sprayed silver to make attractive Christmas decorations. Push long sticks into the fruit and display them in an old metal bucket or basket for a quick Christmas arrangement.

Spices such as peppercorns and nutmegs look wonderful when glued into smaller arrangements.

Cinnamon sticks These are a real must. They smell exotically festive. Bunches of cinnamon sticks tied with rope or simple bows will transform a table. Pile bundles on a small tray, or glass plate and toss some dried fruits around them to create a quick table centrepiece.

Regularly break off a small knob of cinnamon stick. The delicious spice smell will permeate through the room. Place a cinnamon stick bundle in your guest room to create a real Christmas welcome.

Pot pourri You can dry your own rose petals during the year. Toss in some dried mosses and chips of cinnamon sticks for a simple and refreshing homemade pot pourri.

Pasta shells Pasta, especially the large variety, look stunning if sprayed silver or gold and added to an arrangement. Alternatively they can be displayed in a clear glass or jar.

Jelly beans These colourful sweets are wonderful at Christmas. Save little pots and other small containers and fill them to the brim with jelly beans to make lovely gifts.

Essential techniques

In this chapter we show just how easy it is to use materials such as pine cones, nuts and fruits with the help of some wire, spray paints and acrylics. A bowl of everyday fruit can be transformed into glorious exotic materials, likewise nuts, pasta and foliage. Don't be afraid to experiment.

Adding colour

Christmas comes but once a year and it is probably the only time that you are able to go mad with a can of gold or silver spray paint. A solid covering looks rich and substantial, but equally beautiful is a fine metallic glaze which catches the eye.

Gilding nuts and shells

All types of nuts look good sprayed; pecans and walnuts look terrific. Don't worry if they are not completely covered with paint, the natural warmth of the nut colouring is very appealing when it shows through the paint.

Place your nuts or shells into a fairly high-sided cardboard box lined with a sheet of newspaper. Shake the can of paint thoroughly and spray into the box from a distance of about 12in (30cm). Give the box a thorough shake and spray again until the nuts or shells are covered to your taste.

Don't lean over the box too closely while spraying. Always spray outside if possible, or in a well-ventilated room

Gilding fruits, foliage, cones and pots

You will be amazed how beautiful ivy leaves look when gilded. Fresh apples, oranges and lemons are quite stunning. Terracotta pots also work well. Vegetables such as leeks can be made magical with silver or gold. Make sure that all materials are clean and dry – this way you get an even coverage.

Painting terracotta pots

This is a lovely activity to do either with children, or on a grander scale with shop-bought stencils or your own designs. There are no colour or theme restrictions. Spots, stripes, squares, spirals all look fantastic.

Terracotta is very absorbent, so before you start painting, coat the pot with PVA glue to stop the paint from sinking in. Use a thick paintbrush to plaster the pot with a generous layer of PVA glue. Pop the pot into the oven on its lowest setting so it dries quickly. This should take about 15 minutes. You can also simply leave the pot somewhere warm for an hour or so, until the glue has dried to a clear shiny finish. Paint or decorate the pot as required.

Cover a fairly large area with plenty of newspaper and lay out materials.

Spray first one side and, after a few moments, turn over and spray the other side.

Drying fruits

When buying fruits to dry make sure that they are not over ripe and are of a good colour. All citrus fruits, such as oranges, lemons, tangerines, grapefruits and limes, are suitable for drying. Apples, lychees and pomegranates also work well. Almost any fruit with a hard skin which is not too fleshy inside will dry beautifully.

Drying sliced fruit

Always make sure the fruit is sliced evenly, so that the slices take the same amount of time to dry.

1 Lay the fruits out on foil-covered baking trays and set your oven to its lowest temperature. Fan ovens are ideal for this job.

2 Leave fruits drying for approximately 12 hours, turning regularly.

3 Remove the fruits from the oven when dry and firm to the touch. Store in an airtight container until you need to use them.

Alternatively, if you are lucky enough to have plenty of space in your airing cupboard, lay out the sliced fruits on trays, so that they don't overlap, and leave them for up to a week, turning occasionally to stop them from sticking.

Don't make the slices too thick or they will take longer to dry.

Drying whole citrus fruits

Small oranges, lemons and limes work best as whole dried fruits. Larger fruits take too long to dry and their skins become too dark in the process.

1 Split the skin of the citrus fruits with a sharp knife from top to bottom five or six times around the fruit. This allows the air to circulate within the fruit and accelerates the drying process. It also looks very attractive when the fruit is dried.

2 Follow the instructions for drying sliced fruits, but leave in the oven for about 48 hours.

Don't be tempted to speed up the process by increasing the oven temperature – this only leads to darkened skins. Should your fruits become baked and look dull after drying you can revamp them with gold floral spray paint. The result will be a beautiful burnished gold fruit.

Drying lychees and pomegranates

Place the fruits on a foil-covered baking tray and bake at the lowest temperature possible for approximately six hours, or leave overnight.

Wiring fruits, cones and pots

Wiring is a major part of the fixing mechanics in Christmas flower arrangements. A lot of the materials used to make decorative Christmas projects are fairly weighty and need to be attached very firmly. Nothing is worse than seeing an elaborate welcome ring adorning a front door with all its decorations dangling off!

When bending wire, do it quickly, especially when twisting two wires together. If you twist it too slowly the wire can buckle, preventing it from gripping the material.

Wiring pine cones

1 Use a 12in (30cm) medium-gauge
stub wire. Place the wire approximately 1in (2.5cm) from the base of the
cone, with a third of the wire
protruding one side of the cone and
two-thirds the other.

2 Press the shorter wire around the
scales of the cone towards the
longer wire.

3 Take the longer wire and wrap it
once around cone (through the
scales) and twist both wires together.
You can leave the cone natural or spray
it lightly; the effect is gorgeous.

---

*Wire cones fairly tightly so that
they remain secure in the
arrangement.*

Wiring whole fruits

1 Choose which side of the fruit you
would like to display, and push a
medium-gauge 12in (30cm) stub wire
right through the fruit approximately
two thirds of the way down from the
display end.

2 Leave about one-third of the wire
showing on one side and two-
thirds on the other side.

3 Taking the shorter piece of wire,
pull it across to meet the longer
wire and twist it around. The longer
wire can be used to attach the apple to
the arrangement.

If the fruits you are using are fresh and
heavy you will need to use another wire
in the same way, perpendicular to the
first. Twist all the wires together
leaving a long enough piece to thread
into your base.

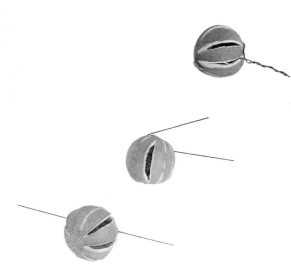

Wiring walnuts

Walnuts are nature's gift to Christmas decoration. They have a tiny hole at the base into which it is possible to slide a 6–8in (15–20cm) medium-gauge stub wire.

1 Hold the walnut at the top and push the wire into the hole at the base of the nut.

2 With a hot glue gun, put a tiny dot of glue to secure the wire. Allow it to dry for a few seconds. Leave the nuts natural or spray them gold if you haven't done so beforehand.

Wiring dried whole fruit

Just tuck the wire in through the slices (which were cut in the fruit prior to drying) to the other side of the fruit and wrap the ends of the wire together as for whole fruit.

Wiring sliced fruits

1 Fan three to five slices and push a medium-gauge 12in (30cm) stub wire through them at the point where they all overlap.

2 Leave one-third of the wire on one side and two-thirds on the other. Twist the shorter wire around the longer one. This leaves the longer wire ready to be inserted into the arrangement.

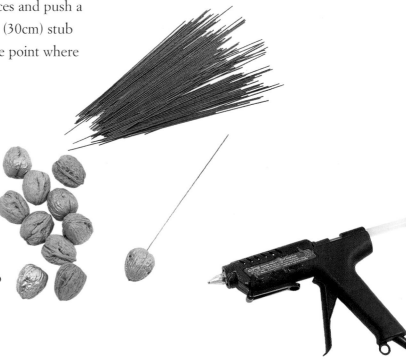

Wiring clay pots

1 Push a 12in (30cm) medium-gauge stub wire through the drainage hole, leaving a third of the wire sticking out of the top of the pot, and two-thirds out of the bottom.

2 Bend the shorter wire down to meet the longer wire approximately halfway down the side of the pot.

3 Twist the shorter wire around the longer one and you have a wired-up pot ready for filling.

Always fill your pot with lichen or moss. This hides the wire inside and looks very attractive. For a more formal touch, tuck a small piece of dry foam inside the pot and glue bright red dried rose heads on to it. If you want to really going to town, line the pot with waterproof material, such as plastic, and then fill the pot with wet foam and fresh flowers.

Cutting foliage

The main types of foliage used in the projects which follow are blue pine and cupressus. Cupressus is cheaper than pine, so for economy's sake use twice as much cupressus as pine in your arrangements.

Blue pine has branches made up of a thick main stem and smaller, finer offshoot branches. Use the offshoot branches, cutting them into 3in (8cm) pieces. Discard the main stem.

Cupressus is made up of a main stem with fine stems branching off it. Starting from the top of the branch cut the main stem into 3in (8cm) portions. Cut from the underside of the branch so that the white of the cut stem is covered by the foliage. This way you won't have to waste any part of the foliage.

Candles

Buy long-burning candles which are non-drip. There is nothing more annoying than having to change your candles half way through a dinner party. Extinguish candles before leaving the room; you can always relight them when you return.

Wiring candles

Your candle needs to be firmly in position before proceeding with an arrangement. If it is wobbly before you start it will definitely be unstable and unsafe by the time you have finished creating the design.

The recipe which follows demonstrates how to wire one candle, but it is worth wiring several at once, and keeping them by until you need them.

You will need:

three 4in (10cm) medium-
    gauge stub wires
florist's tape

1 Bend the wires into three U shapes by hand or using pliers.

2 Holding the candle firmly, place one U-shaped wire against the base the of candle and tape it on. Press the florist's tape over the wire and move a third of the way around the candle and attach the next wire. Proceed in this manner around the candle until the tape meets up and all three wires are firmly attached at evenly spaced intervals.

3 Go once or twice around the candle again with the tape to make sure the wires are firmly secured. The tape needs to sit as close to the base of the candle as possible. This ensures that no tape is visible once the candle project is completed.

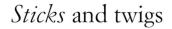

Sticks and twigs

Ordinary twigs from the garden can be used to support decorations which are going to stand up in foam, a vase or a basket. We used the twigs gathered from local woods, but you can also use garden canes, perhaps spraying them gold and silver. Apples and mandarins work well, even some vegetables look great when 'stemmed up' on twigs like this.

Make sure the twigs are dry and firm. Sharpen the end of the twig or stick with a penknife. Push the twig firmly into the fruit, adding a dot of glue where the fruit meets the twig if it feels loose.

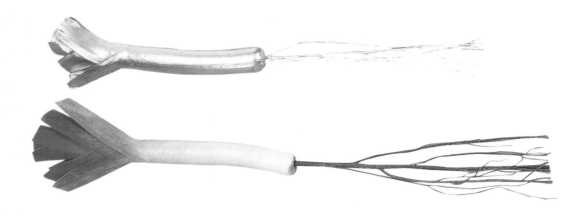

Cinnamon stick bundles

1 Collect together a substantial bundle of sticks making sure that the sticks are roughly the same length.

2 Taking a 12in (30cm) medium-gauge stub wire, hold the sticks in one hand and place the wire underneath with one-third of the wire showing on one side and two-thirds showing on the other.

3 Taking the longer wire, wrap it very tightly around the bundle twice and twist the remaining length of long wire to the short wire. If the sticks are not secure enough and slip around, finish off with a small amount of glue between the sticks.

4 Cover the wire with either ribbon or glue some moss, nuts or dried flowers over the top.

Alternatively, tie the bundles with thin rope or raffia, adding a dot of glue inside the bundle to hold it together.

Mossing a rope

A mossed rope provides a flexible base
for a garland and other simple
arrangements. Rough measurements are
given here, but it is worth checking the
space where you intend to hang your
garland to make sure you make a rope
the correct length.

You will need:

1 length of parcel string, 7ft long
  (about 2m)

2 buckets damp sphagnum moss

1 reel medium-gauge wire

1 Make a loop at both ends of the string. Knot a reel of wire to one end of the string. Start at the left end if you are right handed – and on the right if you are left handed. This wire should remain on the spool until the mossing is finished.

2 Place a small handful of sphagnum moss on the string where the wire is attached and bind the wire around it a couple of times to secure the moss. Continue until all the string is covered and the moss is firmly secured. End by knotting the wire securely and cutting it. You now have a firm moss rope about 2in (5cm) in diameter and 6ft (about 2m) long.

Mossing a welcome ring

Welcome rings need a strong wire base to keep them in shape. The wire frame is an invaluable aid to forming a smooth, uniformly thick moss ring. A mossed ring forms the basis of the blue pine and curly cupressus welcome ring.

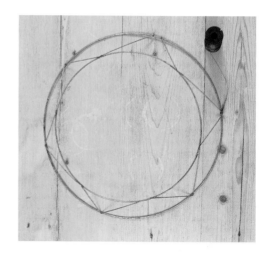

You will need:

Wire ring of the correct size

½ bucket of sphagnum moss

1 reel medium-gauge wire

Carpet moss (optional)

Wire pins (optional)

1 Tie the reel of wire to a point on the wire ring.

2 Place a small handful of sphagnum moss on the ring where the wire is attached and bind the wire around it a couple of times to secure the moss.

Continue until the ring is covered and the moss is firmly secured. End by knotting and cutting the wire.

You will need to add a layer of carpet moss if the ring is not going to be completely covered in some sort of decoration.

The carpet moss is simply pinned onto the sphagnum moss base using wire pins.

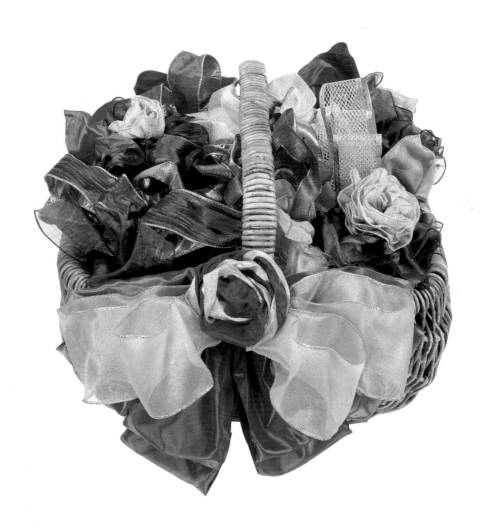

Ribbons
and bows

The finishing touches of an arrangement can be simple or sophisticated. Raffia, hessian and twigs have a more natural and rustic feel. Ribbons are available in a spectacular range of colours, adding glamour and richness. The knots and bows you see here range from the most basic to the fantastically opulent. You can use these finishes on any of the projects which follow – choose the one which suits your mood or the occasion.

Raffia knots

A simple raffia granny knot can be very
effective tied around a pot or vase of
almost any shape. Glue the back of the
knot into position so it sits beautifully
and securely in place.

Twig bow

1 You will need a large pile of thin freshly fallen twig branches about 20in (50cm) long. Old twigs are generally too brittle to shape. Remove any offshoots from the main stem of the twig. Soak the twigs for a few minutes in a large bucket or sink of hot water, pushing them down under the water with a long wooden spoon.

2 Take the twigs out and sort them into groups of five or six. Shape them into a bow, curling the twigs back on themselves until you have achieved the size of bow you require. You don't need to tie a bow, just loop the two ends back into the middle.

3 Attach some gold cord around the very centre of the bow to hold it firmly in shape.

If you require a coloured twig bow, spray the twigs gold and silver before you start. Then, once the bow is made, spray them again. Hang from a hook until dry and then retouch any areas which look patchy.

Ribbons

We prefer to work with wired ribbon; it holds its shape exquisitely and soft bends and curves are formed with ease and speed. These bows will last from year to year, so spending a little extra money and time on them will be a worthwhile investment.

Try to achieve a balanced effect when adding several bows to an arrangement. Make at least three bows in toning colours and group them together. Add a rosebud, made from the same ribbons, to the centre of the arrangement.

Rosebuds

Rosebuds can look magnificent. Practise making them with short pieces of leftover wired ribbons, at least 3in (7cm) wide. You will need about 20in (50cm) of wired ribbon per rosebud. Soft gauzy types are best, the firmer velvet ribbons are too heavy to mould.

1 Hold the ribbon firmly in one hand, gripping the thread wire at the bottom edge of the ribbon. Gently pull the opposite end of the thread wire and allow the body of the ribbon to

pleat and gather. The bottom edge of the ribbon forms the centre of the bud while the top of the ribbon forms the bud petals.

2 You will find that the bud forms quite naturally as you pull the wire thread. Coil the gathered folds of the ribbon carefully into circular folds that twist around on each other.

3 Anchor the end of the wire by taking the wires from the top and bottom of the ribbon and knotting them together, wrapping them around the bottom of the rosebud so that the petals don't come loose. Alternatively you can stitch the bottom layers together. The remaining wire can be used to attach the rosebud.

Save the long piece of fine wire leftover from making the rosebud. It can be used to wire fine ribbons into a cheat's bow.

Twirled two-ribbon rosebud

A very beautiful rosebud can be made from two contrasting ribbons. These are particularly stunning when used as a centre to petal bows.

You will need to practise this method on leftover pieces of ribbon. After a while you will find you can achieve perfect results in minutes.

1 Take about 20in (50cm) of wired gold ribbon and the same length of a contrasting wired ribbon. Hold the ends of both ribbons together. Pull the top wire of the contrasting ribbon wires first, gathering in the ribbon with a gentle pleating effect. Repeat with the gold ribbon, folding it over and around the contrasting ribbon. Continue in this fashion, gently criss-crossing the ribbons over each other as the bud enlarges.

2 Wire the base of the bud to fix it in place if you wish, but a needle and thread works best.

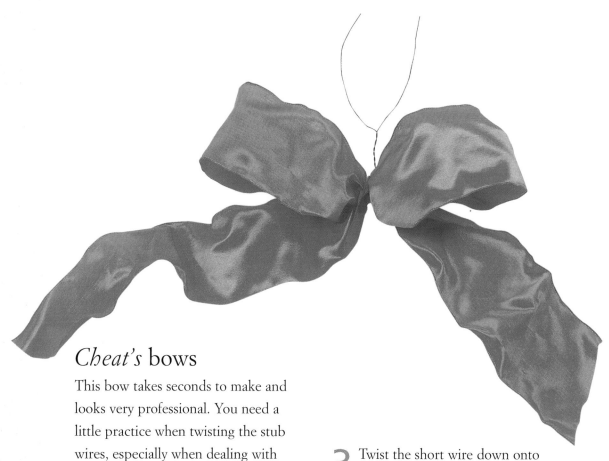

Cheat's bows

This bow takes seconds to make and looks very professional. You need a little practice when twisting the stub wires, especially when dealing with hessian bows, which are heavy and harder to pleat tightly.

1 Take a length of ribbon and fold it into the shape of a bow (see twig bow on page 37).

2 Take a 12in (30cm) length of medium-gauge stub wire (fine gauzy ribbons will need a finer wire). Put the wire behind the bow with one-third showing above the bow and two-thirds below. Take the longer piece of wire and twist it firmly and quickly around the centre of the bow.

3 Twist the short wire down onto the long wire. The long wire can be used to attach the bow to the arrangement.

It is important to twist the wire around the centre of the bow firmly and briskly, so it plumps up the bow creating a three-dimensional effect.

Double petal bows

These are great fun to make and look exceptionally beautiful. The aim is to produce a lovely fluffy double bow, wired firmly in the middle to give it poise. The double bow consists of a front bow, which is about 2in (5cm) or more shorter than the folds of the petals the back bow.

1 Take a length of ribbon (wired ribbon works best) about 50in (1.3m) long. Start by forming the left fold of the front bow. With the right side of the ribbon facing you, fold the end 5in (1.3m) or one-tenth of the length behind the front. Hold the

centre of the bow firmly with thumb and forefinger. Make the other half of the bow, checking that it is the same length as the first. The first front bow should now be complete.

2 Fold the ribbon back on itself again about 2in (5cm) from the centre and make the back bow in the same way as the first. For the final loop of the back bow take the very end of the ribbon and fold it back into the centre as shown, slightly overlapping the central point of the bow.

3 Twist a stub wire tightly around the centre of the bow, leaving a wire long enough to attach it to the arrangement.

Complex petal bows

More complex and luxurious bows can be made from three different double petal bows. Toning colours and soft, gauzy ribbons work best. Use a short length of stub wire to attach the bows together. Finish by wiring a matching rosebud into the centre of the bows.

Many ribbons look superb when the reverse or 'wrong' side of the ribbon is used.

Garlands

Welcome rings

Buckets and logs

Table centrepieces

Candles

Christmas trees

Chairbacks

Gifts for unexpected visitors

Traditional
Christmas Garland

Christmas is a wonderful time to lavish your home with traditional homemade garlands. When creating any type of garland think big and make a statement. This wonderfully abundant evergreen garland can be decorated with anything which catches your eye, or which suits the decorative theme you have chosen.

Making the basic garland

Ingredients

For 6ft (1.8m) of garland

1 length of parcel string 7ft (about 2m) long

Black plastic sheeting to line the back of the garland

2 buckets damp sphagnum moss

6 branches of blue pine, cut into 3in (7.5cm) pieces

12 branches of curly cupressus, cut into 3in (7.5cm) pieces

1 reel of medium-gauge wire

Wire pins

Equipment
Scissors

Preparation time
2½ hours

Refer to
Cutting foliage 26

Mossing a rope 30

1 Cut the cupressus and moss the rope (see pages 26 and 30). Attach a reel of wire at the beginning of the mossed rope. Take three pieces of blue pine and lay them across the mossed rope, making sure that their tips cover the loop at the end of the string. Hold the pine in place and wrap the wire tightly around the stems of the pine – two turns will do.

2 Take three pieces of cupressus and repeat the process, making sure that the twigs of the second bunch overlap the stems of the pine. At each turn, wrap the wire very tightly around the mossed rope. This ensures that nothing will drop out of the garland when you hang it. Take another three pieces of cupressus and repeat the process again.

5 Cut long 4in (10cm) strips of black plastic and pin them along the back of the rope with wire pins to prevent any damp from seeping out of the moss onto wallpaper or polished surfaces.

6 Put the garland outside where it will be cool and dampened by the rain. This will ensure that it stays fresh at least two weeks before you need it. Hang the garland where required, using the loops at the end of the string.

3 Continue in this way until you reach the centre of the rope, then knot and cut the wire. Turning the garland, start the process from the other end, until the other half of the rope is covered. End as before and cut the wire.

4 Wire together two bunches of blue pine and attach them to the centre of the rope. You will need to add some decoration, such as a bow, to cover the join.

1 Put the candles in holders, so that they won't fall over, and place them along the shelf behind the garland. Attach the bows at the middle and corners of the garland as focal points. Push the wire through the garland until it comes through the back of the mossed rope, then bend the wire back on itself into the moss.

2 Attach the cones (groups of three or five), apples (groups of three) and cinnamon sticks at regular intervals, about one every foot (about 30cm). Using a glue gun, glue the pecans and walnuts to the garland in clusters.

Variations

Add champagne corks to the garland after the New Year celebrations. Two groups of five or seven corks wired along with their casings will add a flash of silver. These novel decorations will distract from any drying foliage.

Christmas fruits and ribbons

Ingredients

24 medium pine cones, wired

9 red apples, wired

1 bag pecan nuts, some sprayed gold

1 bag walnuts, some sprayed gold

6 bunches of cinnamon sticks, wired

3 double bows with rosebud centres, wired

5 or 6 large church candles

Refer to

Wiring fruits, cones and pots 22

Cinnamon stick bundles 29

Ribbons and bows 34

Silver Twig Garland

This is a very quick and easy to make garland suitable for framing doorways, fireplaces or gates. It can be enhanced with threads of small fairy lights. It looks stunningly simple with no further decoration.

Ingredients

4 bundles of birch twigs, sprayed silver

Reel of medium-gauge stub wire

3 silver rosebuds with blue net trims

Small large-headed nails

Equipment

Hammer, scissors

Preparation time

1½ hours

Refer to

Ribbons and bows 34

1 Measure the space over which you intend to hang the garland. The twigs you use should be long enough to reach halfway across this space. In the example shown, the twigs were approximately 4ft (120cm) long.

2 Working on a flat surface, gather the twigs into four bundles holding them firmly at one end. Tie the bundles about 3in (7.6cm) from the ends with reel wire as though you are making the brush of a broom. Bind the wire several times around the twigs and fasten the end of the wire off securely.

3 Lay two bundles at right angles to each other as shown. Wire these bunches together with a couple of loops and fasten off. Do the same with the other two bundles of twigs.

4 Knock a couple of small large-headed nails in around the doorway, shelf or mantelpiece where you intend to place the garland. Attach the garland with wire from behind. Using small lengths of reel wire, wire together a couple of twigs in the middle of the garland where the two sets of bunches meet. Wire in the rosebuds.

Don't add too much decoration to this swag as it cannot support nearly as much weight as a moss-based garland. Keep the garland at least 2ft (60cm) from fire

Variations

Use an evergreen such as holly to dress the garland. Here, dried lotus heads were sprayed gold and wired into the silver twigs along with crisp, red velvet double bows.

Gilded Ivy Garland

An ivy garland will add a wonderful evergreen touch to
your home. Spray a few trails gold to add a festive touch.
The green leaves will contrast beautifully with the gilded
trails, creating a warm natural feel.

Ingredients

20 or 30 long trails of ivy

Reel of medium-gauge wire

Twig bow, sprayed gold

Small large-headed nails

Equipment

Scissors, hammer

Preparation time

1 hour

Refer to

Adding colour 18

Ribbons and bows 34

1 Wash the ivy and hang it up to dry in a cool room. When the ivy is dry you can spray selected strands gold.

2 Divide the trails into four bundles, leaving eight individual strands aside. Taking one bundle, arrange the trails so that the cut ends are together. Using reel wire, bind each bundle together firmly and tie it off. Taking two bundles, bind the ends at right angles (see Silver Twig Garland on page 50). Bind the remaining two bundles in the same way.

3 Knock in a couple of small large-headed nails where you intend to build the garland. Attach the bundles to the nails using short lengths of reel wire. Start at the corners of the garland and work inwards. Use the spare trails of ivy to cover the join in the centre of the garland.

Variations

Use more complex bows in toning golden colours to complement the golden ivy trails. This garland has been made from 100 or so trails of ivy to give it dimension. When adding more ivy trails, wire them in behind the framework you have already created.

4 Decorate the centre of the garland with a twig bow, attached with a short piece of reel wire.

Ivy garlands look best if decorated simply, with bows and ribbons, so that the foliage is the focus.

Traditional Christmas
Welcome Ring

Christmas forest fruits – cones, nuts and apples – adorn
rings beautifully. All the ingredients should be top quality
and have wonderful rich colour. Visitors entering your
home will be very close to your creation while waiting on
the doorstep, so take extra care with decorations.

Ingredients

12in (30cm) wire ring,
  mossed with sphagnum moss
1 reel of wire
12in (30cm) medium-gauge
  stub wire, for hanging
3 branches of blue pine
6 branches curly cupressus
6 corks, wired

Preparation time

40 minutes

Refer to

Cutting foliage 26
Mossing a welcome ring 32

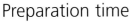

1 Moss the welcome ring using the instructions given on page 32. When you finish mossing the welcome ring, do not tie off the wire reel. Just leave it attached so you can begin binding on the blue pine cupressus.

2 Cut blue pine and cupressus into 3in (7.5cm) pieces, snipping off any damaged or discoloured parts (see page 26).

3 Take three pieces of blue pine and place one in the middle and one either side of the welcome ring. Now bind the reel wire around the stems.

4 Take three pieces of cupressus and do the same as in the previous step, making sure that the tips of the cupressus overlap the stems of the blue pine, covering the woody parts. Take another three pieces of cupressus and repeat the process.

5 Continue all the way around the ring until the foliage covers the mossed ring. End with a couple of turns of the wire and knot as usual. The finished ring should be fluffy but firmly tied down, with no loose foliage.

6 To prevent the ring from marking your door, place the wired corks into the back of the ring. These will hold the ring away from the door.

Christmas fruits and cinnamon sticks

Ingredients

6 apples, wired

3 small bunches of cinnamon sticks, wired and tied with cream ribbon

6 cones, wired and sprayed gold

4 short trails of ivy, sprayed gold

1 small bag of mixed unshelled nuts, glued into two groups and wired to a ribbon bow

Large double petal, dark-green velvet bow

Two cream rosebuds

Refer to

Adding colour 18

Wiring fruits, cones and pots 22

Ribbons and bows 34

Choose which way up you would like the welcome ring. Where you have ended off is the ideal place. Make the stub wire into the hooks and attach it to the ring. Attach a bow to cover the hook. Add the decorations in groups, but try to avoid creating a symmetrical arrangement.

Variations

A less 'fluffy' ring can be created using carpet moss to cover the sphagnum mossed ring (see page 32). This kind of ring will be more structured, drawing attention to the decorations you put on it. Here we used limes, dried mandarins, shells, nuts, cinnamon sticks and beautiful gold and green ribbon.

Silver Twig Ring

Twigs, either left natural or sprayed with paint, form a very natural and stylish ring. This kind of ring suits contemporary decorations in coordinated colours. The ring will not dry out so can be used again and again.

Ingredients

1 large bundle of willow or birch
twigs, 2–3ft (60–90cm) long

Silver spray paint

1 reel wire

12in (30cm) medium-gauge
stub wire, for hanging

Preparation time

1 hour

Refer to

Adding colour 18

1 Soak the twigs in warm water in a
bath or large tub until they are soft
and pliable.

2 Remove them from the water to a
newspaper-covered surface. Start
work straight away, bending the twigs
around into a circle and tying them at
intervals with reel wire. Make sure that
the ring is roughly the same thickness
all of the way around.

3 Work your way around the ring,
using a plate or wire ring frame as
a guide if necessary. Finish off by tying
any ends in securely. Hang the ring up
to dry in a warm place. Do not begin
the next step until the ring is
completely dry.

4 Spray the twig ring thoroughly
with silver spray paint. You may
need two or three coats to get complete
coverage. Decide which way up you
want the ring to hang. Form the length
of wire into a thick hoop and wire it
into the twig ring.

Winter fruits and pots

Ingredients

10 small terracotta pots,
   wired and sprayed silver
4 pomegranates,
   cut in half and wired
6 mandarins, dried and wired
Thin orange gauze ribbon
Large double petal bow in
   toning orange and red
   ribbons

Preparation time

40 minutes

Refer to

Adding colour 18
Drying fruits 20
Wiring fruits, cones and pots 22
Ribbons and bows 34

A silver twig ring, especially a fairly large one as you see here, won't maintain its shape if it is heavily decorated. Use fairly light decorations, arranged evenly around the ring.

Variations

Try leaving the twigs and the ingredients natural. The woody colours of the twigs, terracotta and moss will create a lovely rustic feel. Add wired hydrangea heads instead of ribbon.

Gilded Ivy Ring

An ivy welcome ring is an unusual alternative to the traditional Christmas ring. The evergreen ivy adds a natural touch and has the advantage of being inexpensive and readily available. Ivy trails are very pliable, so the ring will require a stiff twig base which you can either buy or make, or alternatively use a wire frame.

Ingredients

20–30 trails of ivy

Twig ring, about 12in (30cm) in diameter

Reel of medium-gauge wire

12in (30cm) medium-gauge
   stub wire, for hanging

Preparation time

30 minutes

Refer to

Adding colour 18

Silver twig ring 60

1 Wash the ivy thoroughly and leave it to dry. Spray a couple of trails gold and leave them to dry.

2 You can make a twig ring using the instructions in the previous project. Attach the reel wire to the twig ring and take a bunch of ivy trails. Bind the trails securely to the twig ring.

3 Work around the ring, ensuring a good thick coverage of ivy all the way around it. Finish by knotting and cutting the wire. Weave any free trails into the arrangement. Decide which way you want the ring to hang, and attach stub wire, shaped into a loop, to hang it on.

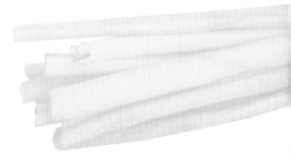

Citrus fruits and golden bows

Ingredients

Three bunches of wired
  cinnamon sticks, bound
  with twine
20 dried limes
10 mandarins sliced and dried
4ft (120cm) length of
  medium-gauge wire
Two golden double bows
  with pulled rosebud centre

Preparation time

45 minutes

Refer to

Drying fruits 20
Cinnamon stick bundles 29
Ribbons and bows 34

Attach the bow at the top of the ring, over the hanging wire. Wire in the cinnamon stick bundles. Make a twist at the end of the medium-gauge wire and thread on the sliced mandarins and dried limes. When all the fruits have been threaded use short lengths of stub wire to attach the fruit rope to the garland.

Variations

Thread whole chilli peppers, bunches of eucalyptus leaves and dried lemon slices on a length of raffia and wind them around the ring.

Thistle Urn

Two dozen cornflower-blue thistles nestle in foam inside a large urn or pot. The pot rim is encircled with a carpet moss ring. This is garnished with groups of wired pomegranate halves and a colourful double petal bow. This decoration will look warm and welcoming on a sideboard.

Ingredients

1 large urn or pot with a lip
   approximately 10–12in
   (25–30cm) in diameter
Plastic to line pot
1 block of wet foam
12in (30cm) wire ring
24 stems fresh blue thistles
9 pomegranate halves, wired
Bowl of sphagnum moss
Carpet moss

Preparation time

40 minutes

Refer to

Wiring fruits, cones and pots 22
Mossing a welcome ring 32

1 Check that the wire ring will rest happily on the rim of the pot. Line the pot or urn with plastic to make it waterproof. Cut the foam block into two, soak it in water and lay both pieces in the urn, side by side or on top of each other.

2 Moss the wire ring with sphagnum moss then cover it with carpet moss (see page 33). Lay the ring carefully on the rim of the urn. Decorate the moss ring with wired pomegranates cut in half. Rich, russet-red groups of three look magical.

3 Strip the lower leaves from the thistles and arrange them in the foam blocks, deeply embedding them in the full depth of the wet foam.

4 Attach a double petal bow to the front of the arrangement and you will have a fabulous display.

By the New Year this piece will have dried. You can refresh any tired elements or, alternatively, replace the fruit with dried flowers, shells or pasta and keep it for the remainder of the year.

Lily Bucket

The exquisite smell of lilies is wonderful at Christmas time. This beautiful arrangement is quick to construct and looks divine. It is best sited in a light, cool corner so the lilies open and last a long time.

Ingredients

1 galvanized bucket,
    10in (25cm) in diameter

1 block wet foam

Plastic to line the bucket

10 stems white lily

¼ bucket damp
    sphagnum moss

Enough carpet moss to
    cover foam surface

Preparation time

20 minutes

1 Place some plastic, such as a discarded plastic carrier bag, inside the bucket and trim it around the top to fit. This will make the bucket waterproof. Fill the bucket half full with sphagnum moss.

2 Immerse the foam block in water for about a minute, or until it is wet through. Cut the block to fit inside the bucket. Make sure the foam is about 1in (2.5cm) from the top of the bucket. This ensures the covering of carpet moss will end up flush with the top of the bucket.

3 Taking one lily at a time, strip off the leaves up to 2in (5cm) from the bottom of the stem.

4 Place a line of lilies in the foam block so that they stand upright, as if growing in the soil, in a straight line from one edge of the foam to the other.

5 Place the remaining lilies into the foam forming a circular arrange-ment. Try to make sure the lilies at the edge of the bucket face outwards. Cover the foam between the lily stems with carpet moss.

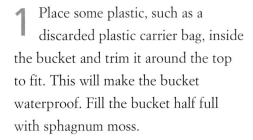

Yuletide Log

This is a fantastically easy project to tackle. It is inexpensive and extremely effective. It adds Christmas cheer to any shelf or mantelpiece and can be made at least two weeks ahead of time.

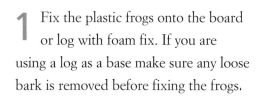

Ingredients

24in (60cm) long board
    or small log

40 wire pins

4 plastic frogs

Small amount of foam fix

1 block dry foam
    (split lengthways in two)

21 pine cones, sprayed gold

7 large deep purple or russet-
    coloured hydrangea heads

2 long ivy trails, sprayed gold

2 large handfuls of
    lichen moss

Equipment

Scissors, glue gun and
    three clear glue sticks

Preparation time

30 minutes

Refer to

Adding colour 18

Wiring fruits, cones and pots 22

1 Fix the plastic frogs onto the board or log with foam fix. If you are using a log as a base make sure any loose bark is removed before fixing the frogs.

2 Split the foam block in two horizontally and place it on top of the frogs. Press it down firmly to secure it in place.

3 If the hydrangea heads do not have a long enough natural stem, make a wire stem by threading an 8in (20cm) fine-gauge wire through the hydrangea floret, twisting it together at the top to make a wire 'stalk'.

Hydrangea heads can sometimes look dull and bleached. A dab of acrylic paint, applied with a paint brush, will add depth and interest to washed-out colours.

4 Insert the cones into the foam in groups of three across the board or log. Thread gold-sprayed ivy trails around and behind the cones, all the way along the arrangement, and fill in any gaps with hydrangea heads and substantial clumps of lichen moss. Make sure that there is no foam showing through when this project is finished.

Variations

Toss small bundles of short cinnamon sticks, tied with raffia or gold ribbon, in and around the cones to add interest. Remove the ivy trails after Christmas and this peaceful arrangement will last indefinitely.

Gold Nut Pot

These chunky nut pots can be made up several weeks in advance of Christmas. They look lovely perched on a sideboard or as a table centrepiece when you have no time to arrange fresh flowers. A candle in the middle can give an extra touch of interest and subtly reflects the gold.

Ingredients

Small bags of unshelled
  hazelnuts, pecans, walnuts
  and brazil nuts
6in (15cm) diameter gold
  sprayed terracotta pot
5¼in (14cm) diameter dry
  foam ball
24in (60cm) long and 1in
  (2.5 cm) wide hesssian gold
  mesh ribbon
Couple of trails of ivy
Wire pins

Equipment

Scissors, glue gun and
  five glue sticks

Preparation time

45 minutes

Refer to

Adding colour 18

1 Spray the pot and three-quarters of the nuts gold. Don't worry if they aren't completely covered; a gold mist can be as effective as a solid gold finish.

2 Using a glue gun, quickly put a few drops of glue around the inside top of the pot and fit the foam ball into it.

3 Using wire pins, pin the hessian ribbon around the foam ball, pleating it every couple of inches. The ribbon forms a skirt around the top of the pot, enabling you to glue the nuts in a random fashion over the side of the pot.

4 Starting at the bottom of the foam and working your way to the top, glue each nut onto the foam ball, forming a gorgeous heap of nuts covering the whole foam surface. It is easier to start with the larger nuts and finish off with the smaller hazelnuts on top. Squeeze the glue onto each nut and not onto the foam.

Variations

5 Bring the nuts over the edge of the pot and down onto the hessian to achieve a cascading effect. Add the gold mesh ribbon, attaching it to the hessian. Tuck ivy leaves firmly around the edge of the foam.

Using the same method, use kidney beans, mixed pulses and sprayed pasta shells. Tie a raffia plait around the edge of the pot and finish it with a contrasting green ribbon.

Mandarin and Pine Cone Centrepiece

This project creates a stunning and imposing festive display. Keep the centrepiece in a cool place until you need to use it, because the mandarins will go off fairly quickly. Choose slightly under-ripe fruit, otherwise you may find the mandarins ripen too quickly.

Ingredients

Approximately 20 small mandarins

Approximately 20 pine cones,
    sprayed gold

Large handful of lichen moss

1 small bag of unshelled pecan
    nuts

1 small bag of unshelled brazil
    nuts

Several wired champagne corks

1 thick church candle, wired

1½ blocks of dry foam

5 plastic frogs

Foam fix

Approximately 25 strong twigs,
    7in (18cm) long

Large plate or terracotta saucer,
    about 20in (50cm) in diameter

Equipment

Scissors, glue gun with two
    clear glue sticks

Refer to

Adding colour 18

Wiring fruits, cones and pots 22

Wiring candles 26

1 If you are using a terracotta saucer, spray it gold and secure frogs to it using foam fix.

2 Place and fix the blocks of foam on top of each other using a twig inserted into each block. Place these securely on top of the frogs. Place a wired candle in the centre of the foam.

You have to be fairly methodical when working on this project to ensure that you end up with a properly balanced look.

3 Stem up the mandarins by inserting
  a twig into the centre of each fruit.
Leave about 3in (7.5 cm) of twig
sticking out of each fruit.

4 Starting at the base of the
  arrangement insert the mandarins
into the foam. Add wired cones using
the wires as 'stems'. Glue on nuts,
randomly filling any gaps and, lastly,
wire in the champagne corks. Fill any
gaps which are left by tucking in
softened lichen moss.

*Keep turning the container so
that you can check you are
achieving an all-round
shape.*

Christmas Rose Loaf

It is a Celtic tradition for a loaf to be brought into the house at midnight on New Year's Eve. What a dazzling surprise to give a rose loaf – a loaf tin edged with moss and packed full of roses. If you prefer, dried roses can be substituted for the fresh roses.

Ingredients

1 loaf tin

Block of wet foam to fit

Plastic for lining tin

20 roses (short stemmed
  will do)

Approximately 3ft (1m) of
  wired silk ribbon

Carpet moss

Equipment

Scissors, glue gun with clear
  glue stick to attach ribbon

Preparation time

20 minutes

Refer to

Ribbons and bows 34

1 Line the loaf tin with plastic. Trim the lining carefully around the top so that it doesn't show.

2 Soak a foam block and then cut it to fit the tin. The foam should fit snugly into your container.

3 Cut the rose stems to about 2in (5cm) and neatly place them into the wet foam in straight lines until the whole tin is full of glorious rose heads. Stuff carpet moss around the edges of the loaf tin. The moss will soften the hard edge of the tin.

4 Glue the wired ribbon to the front of the loaf tin using the glue gun and a clear glue stick.

Choose fresh roses which are of good colour and unmarked.

Variations

Here, a silk tube of ribbon, in shot tones of pale lavender and pink, has been filled with tiny dried rose heads. The tube is hung from the corners of the tin, and attached with tiny pieces of florists tape. This creates a delightful swag of trapped roses on each side of the loaf tin, so that the arrangement looks wonderful from all sides.

After using the arrangement, place it in a warm place to dry. If you are lucky the rose heads will dry in the tin. Replace the moss from time to time and change the bow to a raffia one. You will then have a lovely dried rose arrangement for the rest of the year.

Try to arrange the flowers so that they are as straight as possible – the impact is wonderful.

Christmas Name Places

Instead of having plain place cards why not make up some of these enchanting little dried rose pots and use them as place setting holders. They look quite adorable nestling between the other festive table decorations. They can be made up well ahead of time and used throughout the year for other celebrations and special dinners.

Ingredients

Terracotta pots
    2in (5cm) diameter
¼ block dry foam
10 small red dried rose
    heads per pot
Carpet or lichen
    moss to finish

Equipment

Glue gun with two
    clear glue sticks

Preparation time

5 minutes each

These little pots need to be crammed with roses to look generous and welcoming. Use strongly coloured roses – Christmas red is ideal

1 Cut the dry foam block into pieces which will fit inside the terracotta pots. Place the foam in the pots and trim it flush with the top of the pots.

2 Insert the stems of the roses into the foam to form two straight lines across the middle of the pot. This leaves a tiny rose-free strip in which you can insert the name card.

3 Fill the remainder of the pot with rose heads, gluing them in where necessary. You will need to do this if the roses haven't got a stem.

4 Push a little carpet or lichen moss around the top of the pot.

Variations

If time is not at a premium, try using wet foam and fresh rose heads instead. Alternatively, fill the pots with clear plastic and spoonfuls of jelly beans. The jelly beans will hold a name place card well and everyone enjoys a sweet finish to a meal. Cinnamon stick bundles tied with small double petal bows also make fantastic name places.

Vine Leaf Candles

A candle enveloped in a vine leaf and wrapped in a criss-cross tie of raffia will transform a table setting. The raffia looks elegant if left on, but can also be removed when the leaf has dried. Vine leaf candles should be prepared in autumn when the vine leaves have turned red. The rich burgundy colours are ideal for the Christmas season.

Ingredients

Fresh vine leaves

Candles

Equipment

Glue gun and clear glue sticks

Preparation time

2 minutes each

1 Choose a large enough leaf
so that it meets and slightly
overlaps around the candle.
Snip off the back of the central
stem without breaking the
surface of the leaf. Wrap it
around the base of the candle.

2 Dot small amounts of glue
onto the candle to fix the
leaf and allow a few moments
for the glue to set.

*Slightly stretch each leaf as you
guide it around the candle –
this gives a beautiful
smooth finish.*

Variations

Instead of using glue, try tying your leaf
with a raffia plait, garden twine, a
Christmas bow or simply a length of
parcel string. Experiment with other
leaves such as red cabbage leaves.

Ivy and Pomegranate

A dazzling, natural but inexpensive arrangement which can stand on a dining room table, sideboard or coffee table. The ivy can be variegated, plain green or sprayed gold.

Ingredients

20 stems of variegated ivy

6 pomegranates, halved

Terracotta saucer, approximately
10in (25.5cm) in diameter

3 plastic frogs

1 block of wet foam

1 wired church candle,
    with vine leaf

Small amount foam fix

Gold floral spray paint

Equipment

Glue gun, florist's scissors

Preparation time

20 minutes

Refer to

Adding colour 18

Wiring fruits, cones and pots 22

Wiring candles 26

Vine leaf candles 85

1 Spray the terracotta saucer gold and leave it to dry. Apply small amounts of foam fix to the base of the terracotta saucer and press on the frogs.

2 Soak the foam block for a minute until it is wet through. Place the wet foam on top of the frogs and press it down firmly into position. Trim the foam to fit if necessary. Position the candle firmly in the centre of the foam.

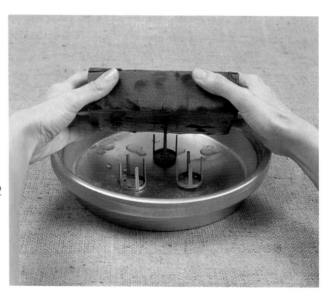

Do not push the stems too far into the foam as this restricts the water supply.

3 Cut the stems of ivy and arrange them around the candle. Position the wired pomegranates in triangles around the arrangement in four separate groups.

Try not to make the arrangement too sprawling if space is at a premium.

Variations

If ivy is not available any lush green foliage will do, although it is a good idea to try and use seasonal foliage such as holly or spruce.

Christmas Hydrangea Pot

Three thin altar candles stand in a terracotta pot,
surrounded by moss. The lip of the brim is covered with
a rope of hay and decorated with groups of delicate dried
hydrangea florets, dried roses, nigella and clusters of
nutmegs sprinkled with dried chopped apple, all
interlocked with laurel leaves.

Ingredients

10in (25.5cm) diameter
   terracotta pot

Dry hard or modelling clay

Plastic lining, for the pot

3 candle holders

Length of twine

2 large handfuls of hay

2 handfuls of lichen or carpet moss

28 dried rose heads

2 whole dried hydrangea heads
   of a strong reddish colour

20 whole nutmegs

16 small laurel leaves, no more
   than 2in (5cm) long and
   1in (2.5cm) wide

4 slices dried apple, chopped

12 dried nigella heads

Equipment

Glue gun and four clear glue
sticks, scissors

Preparation time

1 hour

Refer to

Candles 26

1   Place a small piece of moss at the bottom of the pot to conceal the drainage hole. Line the pot with plastic, trimming around the top.

2   Pack the dry hard or modelling clay (plaster of Paris cannot be used) into the terracotta pot, leaving approximately 1in (2.5cm) free at the top.

3   Insert the candle holders into the centre of the dry hard to form a circle. Alternatively you can wire the candles (see page 26) and stick them directly into the foam.

4 Take a large handful of hay and gently tease it into a 2in (5cm) wide rope. Using the twine, tie the hay every 1½ in (3–4cm) to secure it, adding more hay if required. The hay rope should be long enough to wrap around the circumference of the pot's rim.

5 Fit the hay rope around the rim of the pot, to check it for size. Join the ends with a further piece of twine.

6 Using a glue gun, place a few dots of glue around the top of the pot, approximately ½in (1.3cm) from the lip and slide the hay ring up the pot, rolling it over the glue dots. Hold it for a few moments until it fixes in place. You should now have a good firm hay base around the top of the pot onto which you will be able to fix your ingredients. Trim stray pieces of hay into a neat band.

7 Using a glue gun, glue a laurel leaf vertically over the hay (apply the glue to the leaf and not to the hay). Glue on another leaf to overlap with the first.

8 Glue on a group of seven rose heads mingled with three nigella heads and a few hydrangea florets (arrange these in a circle to cover the hay). Glue on two more overlapping laurel leaves.

9 Glue a group of five nutmegs and fill in the gaps between the nuts with pieces of chopped dried apple. Glue on two further overlapping leaves.

Different groups of flowers should sit opposite each other around the pot. When you have finished all the hay should be covered. material.

Continue around the pot in this way, making sure that you divide the flower and nutmeg groups with overlapping leaves, until the pot rim is beautifully adorned.

Finish by pressing carpet moss or lichen over the top of of the clay, covering the candle holders. Replace the moss from time to time to freshen up the arrangement.

Rose and Ivy

A chunky church candle nestled amongst roses and ivy is a spectacularly beautiful centrepiece for Christmas Eve. It is surprisingly simple to put together; circular groups of roses are popped into the foam in groups of five or seven and ivy trails are trimmed to fill the gaps.

Ingredients

8in (20cm) diameter
    terracotta pot
Plastic to line the pot
½ block of wet foam
Sphagnum moss
1 thick church candle,
    approximately 3in (7.6cm)
    wide and 8in (20cm) high
3–4in (9–10cm) long
    medium-gauge stub wires
Florist's tape
28 fresh rose heads
8 fresh dark green ivy trails

Equipment

1 pair of scissors

Preparation time

25 minutes

Refer to

Vine leaf candles 85
Wiring candles 26

 1 Place a tiny piece of sphagnum moss inside the bottom of the pot to cover the drainage hole. Line the pot with plastic and trim it flush with the top of the pot.

2 Cut the foam block to fit, allowing approximately 2in (5cm) to show above the top of the terracotta pot.

3 Pack remainder of sphagnum moss around the foam block to make sure it is wedged in.

4 Take the wired candle and place it in the centre of the foam, making sure it is completely secure.

5 Cut the rose stems to about 2in (5cm). Insert the roses into the foam starting at the top near the candle. Form a glorious dense circle or triangle of roses using seven heads.

6 Repeat these groups of roses around the pot in four sections and fill the gaps with trails of Christmas ivy. Top the pot up with warm water daily to ensure that the arrangement lasts.

Cut the roses for the top of the pot slightly shorter than those at the bottom to avoid a squashed look. If possible use roses that are well open and not tight buds.

Shaker Tree

Although the idea of a Shaker tree is one of simplicity, you can achieve stunning effects using plain decorations. Groups of natural materials such as moss-filled terracotta pots and apples look great. See how we have hidden the trunk with apples and ivy – giving the tree a beautiful woodland look.

Ingredients

Pine Christmas tree

Long trails of dark green ivy

Groups of wired apples

Sphagnum moss

Hessian bows

Bundles of cinnamon sticks, wired

Tiny terracotta pots, wired and
  filled with moss

A long string of clear fairy lights

Preparation time

1 hour

Refer to

Wiring fruits, cones and pots 22

Ribbons and bows 34

1 Make sure the tree is securely placed in the bucket or pot you intend to use. Wrap the trunk with dark green ivy trails, wiring them directly onto the trunk.

2 Decorate the tree with tiny clear fairy lights. (Not strictly in the Shaker style, these lights highlight the subtle colours of the foliage.) Make sure the lights are evenly spaced across the tree.

3 Decorate the tree with hessian bows, tiny wired terracotta pots filled with lichen moss, bundles of cinnamon sticks, wired apples and other Shaker-style decorations.

Bring the undecorated tree inside at the last minute to avoid premature drying. Stand it in a bucket of wet sand to help keep it fresh.

Silver Twig Tree

This is a stunning alternative to the traditional Christmas tree. Here we have enhanced the silver twigs with glorious golden apples and silver leeks. The tree is finished with gold-sprayed netting at the base, filled with golden cones. As the final touch, a large gold twig bow perches at the front.

Ingredients

1 large metal container or bucket

3 dry foam blocks

Large armful of silver sprayed
    twigs, approximately 5ft 5in
    (1.5 metres) tall

1 dozen apples, sprayed gold and
    stemmed up on long canes

10 large cones, sprayed gold

10 leeks, sprayed gold and
    stemmed up on long canes

1 large gold twig bow

Sphagnum moss

Wire to secure base netting

Willow netting or chicken wire
    sprayed gold

Preparation time

40 minutes

Refer to

Adding colour 18

Sticks and twigs 28

Ribbons and bows 34

1 Place the foam blocks inside the container, one on top of the other and pack sphagnum moss around the sides to secure it in place.

2 If the twigs are unruly, train them by tying them in the middle with twine and leave them for a day or two. When released the twigs will look dense and keep their shape. Trim off stray stems and touch up the exposed twig with silver paint. Arrange the twigs in the container

3 Arrange the apples and leeks in the middle of the twigs, placing them so that when they swing out they arrange themselves in a balanced fashion.

Let the natural colours of the apples and leeks show through the paint, adding a touch of natural colour.

4 Twist and coil the netting around the base of the twig arrangement, wiring both ends together. Fill the coils with gold-sprayed cones. Wire on the twig bow to finish.

Try to avoid making this project too wild and unruly as it will take up too much room for the everyday home.

Mandarin and Nut Ball Chairback

These are an impressive treat for friends or family at
Christmas time. Chairbacks add interest in a simple
kitchen or a formal dining room. Use them to
complement your table arrangements.

Ingredients

4in (10cm) length of fine-gauge
stub wire

5in (13cm) diameter dry
    foam ball

Length of wired gold ribbon

2 yards (2m) of wide mesh
    ribbon to decorate

5 whole dried and wired
    mandarins

5 groups of dried apple
    slices, wired

Small bag of unshelled pecan
    nuts, hazelnuts, walnuts and
brazil nuts, sprayed gold

Carpet or lichen moss

Equipment

Scissors, glue gun with five
    clear glue sticks

Preparation time

40 minutes

Refer to

Adding colour 18
Drying fruits 20
Wiring fruits, cones and pots 22

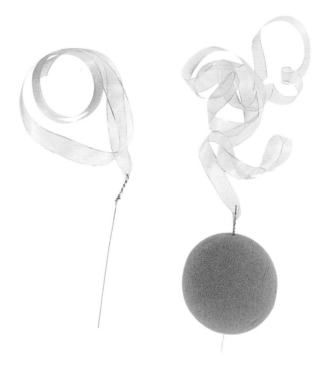

1 Attach the ribbon to the fine-gauge
    wire and push the wire through the
middle of the foam ball and out the
other side.

2 Working on a flat surface, place five
    of the dried and wired mandarins
around the circumference, putting one
in the middle of the foam ball. Fill in the
spaces between the mandarins with the
golden nuts using a hot glue gun. Add
the apple slices as you go. You will only
need to fill the front two thirds of the
ball as the back will rest against the back
of the chair.

3 Fill any gaps that are left on the foam with lichen or carpet moss. Cover the back of ball by gluing on carpet or lichen moss.

4 Use the fine ribbon to attach the arrangement to a chair. You can add a wire mesh bow behind the arrangement. Here, two ribbons were hung from the chair and tied together to make a double bow.

As every ingredient used is dried, this project can be made up well in advance and stored carefully prior to use.

Evergreen Berry, Fruit and Cone Chairback

These chairbacks are best made the day before and allowed to drain. You can add fresh bright Christmas roses or any other flower of your choice to make further impact.

Ingredients

Medium-size wet foam pan

4in (10cm) length of fine-
gauge stub wire for
threading ribbon

1 length fine gold ribbon for
hanging

7 sprigs flowering laurus steinus

5 sprigs rose hips (or similar
berried foliage)

5 bunches of crab apples
with foliage

5 sprigs variegated euonymus

5 wired cones

3 dried and wired
whole mandarins

Equipment

Scissors

Preparation time

30 minutes

Refer to

Drying fruits 20
Wiring whole fruits 23

1 Soak the foam pan in water for about
four minutes and allow to drain.

2 Twist the fine-gauge wire onto one
end of the fine ribbon and thread
through the back of the foam pan.
Some 'pew-end pans', as they are
sometimes called, have a handle with a
hole at the top through which the
ribbon can be threaded if required.

3 Working on a flat surface insert the
laurus steinus around the
circumference of the pan using a
slightly longer piece for the bottom.

4 Working towards the centre of the pan, fill the space with the various green ingredients, rose hips and crab apples, using shorter stems as you get nearer to the centre.

5 When you are happy with the shape and size of your arrangement finish by inserting the cones and mandarins using the wires as stems.

6 Attach the arrangement to the back of the chair with the fine ribbon.

Variations

Use bright double bows around the chairback to give an extra festive touch. Artificial fruits, such as cherries and crab apples, work well with fresh foliage.

Gifts for Unexpected Visitors

There are always a few of these! What could be easier than popping a heap of brightly coloured jelly beans into a galvanized bucket, lined with clear cellophane. Tie the handle with a bright Christmas ribbon.

These gifts are creative, inexpensive and don't smack of a last minute anything-will-do present! Wire up some foiled sweets and arrange in a gold-sprayed terracotta pot, add moss and finish with a bow.

About the authors

Carol Cox, born in the United Kingdom, studied art in Italy. She then started a highly successful flower and plant company in London which she ran herself for many years. Carol leads a busy life – she is involved in a variety of charities and gives flower workshops and school demonstrations. She is mad about horses, art, sport and reading. Carol is married and has three children: Bex, Woody and Georgina, as well as two stepchildren. She lives in Fulham in London.

Josie Cameron-Ashcroft, born in New Zealand, studied education in Dunedin and psychology at London University, followed by photography and design. She started a flourishing co-educational independent school of which she remains the principal. Her passions embrace opera, underwater photography and flowers. She lives in the heart of the Oxfordshire countryside and has three children: Lucy, Henry and Edward. Her country garden often provides inspiration and materials for flower designs and arrangements.

Index

acrylic paints 3

berries 4, 107-9
blue pine 26
bows 36-7, 40-3, 65
buckets 13, 69-70

candle holders 5
candles 26-7, 85-96
centrepieces 74-84
chairbacks 103-9
cheat's bow 40-1
chicken wire 2
Christmas trees 97-102
cinnamon sticks 15, 29, 59
circular wire ring 2
citrus fruits 15, 21, 65
colour 18-19
complex petal bows 43
cones see pine cones
corks 13
cupressus 26
cutting foliage 26

double petal bows 42-3
dry hard 4
drying fruits 20-1

equipment 2-5
evergreen berry, fruit and cone
    chairback 107-9
evergreen foliage 8

florist's scissors 5
florist's tape 4
foam blocks/balls 3-4
foam fix 5
foliage 8, 18-19, 26
fruits 15, 49, 59, 62, 107-9
    citrus 15, 21, 65
    drying 20-1
    spraying 18-19
    wiring 23-4

galvanized buckets 13
garlands 46-55
gifts for unexpected visitors 111
gilded ivy garland 53-5
gilded ivy ring 63-5
glass vases 13

glue 3
glue gun 4, 5
glue sticks 5
gold nut pot 74-6
gravel 4

holly 7
hydrangea pot 90-3
hydrangeas 6

ivy 7, 53-5, 63-5, 94-6
ivy and pomegranate candle
    87-9

jars 13
jelly beans 15, 111
jelly moulds 13

lichens 9
lily bucket 69-70
loaf tins 13
lychees, drying 21

mandarin and nut ball
    chairback 103-6
mandarin and pine cone
    centre-piece 77-9
materials 6-16
mosses 9
mossing 30-3
mossing wire 2

name places 83-4
nuts 8, 15, 18, 24, 74-6, 103-6

paint brushes 3
paints 3
parcel string 3
pasta shells 15
pebbles 11
pine cones 8, 18-19, 23, 77-9,
    107-9
plaster of Paris 4
plastic berries 4
pomegranates 21, 87-9
pot pourri 15
pots 13, 18-19, 25, 62
pulses 15
PVA glue 3, 19

raffia knot 36

reel wire 2
ribbons 38-43, 49
rings see welcome rings
rose and ivy candle 94-6
rose loaf 80-2
rosebuds 38-9
roses 6

scissors, florist's 5
seeds 15
Shaker tree 97-9
shells 11, 18
silver twig garland 50-2
silver twig ring 60-2
silver twig tree 100-2
snake, mossing a 30-1
    see also garlands
spices 15
    see also cinnamon sticks
spray painting 18-19
spray paints 3
sticks 28-9
    see also twigs
string 3
stub wires 2

table centrepieces 74-84
tape, florist's 4
terracotta pots 13, 19
thistle urn 66-8
twig bow 37
twigs 10, 28-9, 50-2, 60-2, 100-2
twine 3
twirled two-ribbon rosebud 39

unexpected visitors,
    gifts for 111

vases 13
vine leaf candles 85-6
vine leaves 10

walnuts 24
welcome rings 56-65
    mossing 32-3
wire pins 3
wire ring 2
wiring 22-5, 26-7

Yuletide log 71-3

GMC Publications

CRAFTS

American Patchwork Designs in Needlepoint	*Melanie Tacon*
A Beginners' Guide to Rubber Stamping	*Brenda Hunt*
Celtic Cross Stitch Designs	*Carol Phillipson*
Celtic Knotwork Designs	*Sheila Sturrock*
Celtic Knotwork Handbook	*Sheila Sturrock*
Collage from Seeds, Leaves and Flowers	*Joan Carver*
Complete Pyrography	*Stephen Poole*
Contemporary Smocking	*Dorothea Hall*
Creating Knitwear Designs	*Pat Ashforth & Steve Plummer*
Creative Doughcraft	*Patricia Hughes*
Creative Embroidery Techniques Using Colour Through Gold	*Daphne J. Ashby & Jackie Woolsey*
The Creative Quilter: Techniques and Projects	*Pauline Brown*
Cross Stitch Kitchen Projects	*Janet Granger*
Cross Stitch on Colour	*Sheena Rogers*
Decorative Beaded Purses	*Enid Taylor*
Designing and Making Cards	*Glennis Gilruth*
Embroidery Tips & Hints	*Harold Hayes*
Glass Painting	*Emma Sedman*
An Introduction to Crewel Embroidery	*Mave Glenny*

Making and Using Working Drawings for Realistic Model Animals	*Basil F. Fordham*
Making Character Bears	*Valerie Tyler*
Making Greetings Cards for Beginners	*Pat Sutherland*
Making Hand-Sewn Boxes: Techniques and Projects	*Jackie Woolsey*
Making Knitwear Fit	*Pat Ashforth & Steve Plummer*
Natural Ideas for Christmas: Fantastic Decorations to Make	*Josie Cameron-Ashcroft & Carol Cox*
Needlepoint: A Foundation Course	*Sandra Hardy*
Pyrography Designs	*Norma Gregory*
Pyrography Handbook (Practical Crafts)	*Stephen Poole*
Ribbons and Roses	*Lee Lockheed*
Rubber Stamping with Other Crafts	*Lynne Garner*
Sponge Painting	*Ann Rooney*
Tassel Making for Beginners	*Enid Taylor*
Tatting Collage	*Lindsay Rogers*
Temari: A Traditional Japanese Embroidery Technique	*Margaret Ludlow*
Theatre Models in Paper and Card	*Robert Burgess*
Wool Embroidery and Design	*Lee Lockheed*

UPHOLSTERY

Seat Weaving (Practical Crafts)	*Ricky Holdstock*
The Upholsterer's Pocket Reference Book	*David James*
Upholstery: A Complete Course (Revised Edition)	*David James*

Upholstery Restoration	*David James*
Upholstery Techniques & Projects	*David James*

HOME & GARDEN

Bird Boxes and Feeders for the Garden	*Dave Mackenzie*
The Birdwatcher's Garden	*Hazel & Pamela Johnson*
Home Ownership: Buying and Maintaining	*Nicholas Snelling*

The Living Tropical Greenhouse: Creating a Haven for Butterflies	*John & Maureen Tampion*
Security for the Householder: Fitting Locks and Other Devices	*E. Phillips*

MAGAZINES

THE DOLLS' HOUSE MAGAZINE ◆ CREATIVE CRAFTS FOR THE HOME ◆ WATER GARDENING

The above represents a selection of related titles currently published or scheduled to be published.
All are available direct from the Publishers or through bookshops, newsagents and specialist retailers.
To place an order, or to obtain a complete catalogue, contact:

GMC Publications, Castle Place, 166 High Street, Lewes, East Sussex BN7 1XU, United Kingdom
Tel: 01273 488005 Fax: 01273 478606
Orders by credit card are accepted